1

Bob's *"AUTO"* Biography

SunBurst Publications

Robert T. Tauber, PhD

[KDP Bobs Cars 4 14 21]

Introduction

I owe my wife, Cissie, for the catchy title inserting the word "AUTO" as in autobiography! After she suggested it, it sounded so obvious.

Does the car make the man or does the man simply make car choices? What does it say to have had an MGA, two MGBs, one MGB-GT, a TR-6 and a Mazda Miata with pop-up headlights? Is it some kind of obsession? If so, I wish everyone shared this same obsession.

What does it say when the author's auto choices evolved into more family oriented vehicles such as Subarus, Hondas and Toyotas - from sedans to a variety of vans and SUVs? A couple of RVs are tossed in, too.

Review approximately 40 vehicles, along with human interest stories of how these autos impacted the author's life - from British sports cars and a VW Bug, to an original Scion xB, a 1988 Cadillac Sedan DeVille, a VW Westphalia camper and a Roadtrek 190 RV.

To the author these autos are a personal museum of memories. For others, cars are just a mode of transportation to get from Point A to Point B. In either case, cars are a reflection of one's personality.

It would have been nice to display these vehicles in their original colors – e.g., British Racing Green for the Miata and bright red for the various British cars. But, for the paperback version. the expense would have been too great.

At one time we had six vehicles including an MGB-GT, a TR-6, a VW Westphalia, a Subaru 4WD, a Saturn, and a Cadallic Sedan DeVille. Somehow we made room to keep them all under roof!

The autos that make up Bob's "AUTO" biography are not presented in chronological order but, instead, are presented by groupings or categories – sports cars, vans, SUVs.

Several of the vehicles will have information about them that requires a second or third page, while others will need just the page where the picture appears.

Although I repeatedly use "I," as in "I bought such and such car…," most often it should be "we" – my wife, Cecelia, and I. Except for the purchase of my first MGB, Cissie was always involved in any and all of our auto purchasing.

The picture on the cover was taken in front of the "Mansion" at Penn State Erie – The Behrend College. Behrend College was named for Otto Behrend who started Hammermill Paper Company on the shores of Lake Erie. When he died, his wife called Penn State and said I have a deal for you. I will give you our summer home (mansion), the outbuildings, and approximately 600 acres of land on the condition that you name the campus for my husband – hence Behrend College

I taught at Behrend College for 25 years while it matured from a 2-year campus into a 4-year college. It currently offers a small college atmosphere while enjoying all of the benefits of being part of The Pennsylvania State University.

Please enjoy sharing this walk down Bob's "auto" lane! Thanks ahead of time.

Robert T. Tauber, PhD
rtt1453@comcast.net

MGA

Cissie and I had given up our jobs as a teacher and guidance counselor in the McKeesport Area School District, and moved to State College, PA, for Bob to pursue his PhD and Cissie to complete her master's degree. We had this car and our VW Bug.

There is art in the flowing design of this car. There is music in the sound of the exhaust. There is a feel as one realizes that the suspension was never designed for a soft, floaty, ride. There is a smell (mostly good) as one rides in a convertible that is so close to the ground.

Cissie and I traveled with Dubby, our Irish Setter, back and forth from State College, PA, to Indian Lake. Not a lot of room for two adults, a large dog and luggage. Dubby found a place to curl up down by Cissie's legs.

While traveling in Irwin, PA, I lost a rear wheel along Route 30 – it just came off and "passed me." Following some earlier body work, the auto body man had neglected to tighten the lug nuts! No serious damage. Sold the car to buy property in Ligonier, PA.

Cissie and I would put the top down and replace it with a tonneau cover. The cockpit cover had "holes" for our heads to stick out as we cruised the mountains around State College on cool fall and winter nights! It was brisk. It was invigorating. It was wonderful!

When the top was up, the wind still blew into and through the car because it did not have wind-up windows but, instead, had Plexiglas sliders. To open the car from the outside one had to slide open one of the sliders, reach in feeling for a cable that was "inside" the door cavity, and pull it. Of course, there was no way to actually lock the car.

The car was, to say the least, a bit low to the ground, which made traveling in snow a challenge. Having said that, it was light enough that a simple "push" could get it unstuck and on its way.

MGB

Purchased the car new in 1965 from Reynold's MG on route 30, Irwin, PA. Was "cool" to drive. The price was $3600 – just about my entire year's salary when I first started teaching!

I almost bought a V-8, Mercury Comet, automatic shift, convertible with red bucket seats. It was red, too. But something told me to buy the "little" red sports car.

Do you know what the M and G in MG stands for? One might think that it was an abbreviation for something "sexy." Actually, it stood for Morris Garage!

I had the MGB when Cissie and I married, whereby we then sold her 1966, 4-on-the-floor, Mustang convertible. Both MGBs that we had (one new that I bought before getting married and one used) were red, with black leather interior and red piping seat trim.

Over Easter I would drive to the junior high school where I taught with a blown-up-bunny in the passenger's seat. It got a laugh. Yes, I made sure that the bunny had on his seatbelt! No, I never tried to use him to take advantage of the HOV (High Occupancy Lane) lanes on a highway,

While living in McKeesport, PA, I would travel back and forth to West Virginia University in Morgantown, West Virginia, while taking graduate classes for my master's degree.

Friends, Steve Tomaino and Fuzzy Knight, also had MGBs – one white and one black. We took turns driving to WVU. This is not all that strange, BUT then you realize that MGs only had two seats with a modest package ledge behind these seats. The three of us took turns being "squeezed" in on the parcel shelf – 65 miles one way!

The top consisted in a two-piece folding tubular structure that, once in place, was then covered with a canvas top that snapped in place. This was all necessary so that the top could be "condensed" and stored in the trunk. Often, I was asked, "How long does it take you to put up the top?" My answer was, "It depends on how hard it was raining!"

Between graduating from college and getting married, I lived with my parents. When I took my mother for a ride and she tried to get into the car while it was parked along a curb, she would say that it was like trying to bend down and get into her oven.

MGB-GT

I purchased this car from Phil Rewers, a local Erie, PA, principal. Great car due, in part, because the windshield was higher than in MGB convertibles This allowed me to avoid having to slouch below the top of the windshield to see down the road.

After spending a 10 month, 1984, sabbatical at Durham University in England, I returned home, along with wife, Cissie, son, David and daughter, Rebecca. Accompanying us were the 18 pieces, yes 18 pieces, of luggage that we had taken there. You might ask, "What does this have to do with an

MGB-GT?" Believe it or not, we also brought home two complete front fenders for the MG! And, there was no charge as we had used a new airline at the time, *Peoples Express*!

At one point, with two active teenage drivers in the house, we had six vehicles. The problem was where to put the MGB-GT for the harsh winter months. The solution was to take the shed we had in the back yard and cut out the rear wall such that the "nose" of the MG could stick into that part. From the outside and rear of the shed it simply looked like a shed protrusion where firewood might be stored inside. It worked!

My son, David, has the car now. To my knowledge he has taken bits and pieces of it apart, has them stacked, ready for restoration.

Ford Mustang

When Cissie and I got married, she had a V-8, 4-on-the-floor, 1966 Ford Mustang convertible. At the time, we had both my 1965 MGB and Cissie's car. Something had to go. It would be great, personally and financially, to have that car now.

One day while riding along in our MG, we happened to see the car wash boy, the son of the local garage owner where we had taken our car to get washed, taking a joy ride in our Mustang. Can't really blame him! I suppose he was just trying to dry off the car. Ha Ha.

A few decades later, #1 grandson has his own Mustang. But his was just a peddle-car version!

TR-6

Coolest car ever! Whereas MGs were rather civilized in looks, comfort and ride, TR-6s were muscle looking and harsh riding. It was claimed that the engine used had its origins in English farm tractors. It was cool in both looks and sound.

I bought it from a local Erie, PA, principal. It had a nice set of distinctive "red line" (versus white wall) tires. Should have kept this car. Becky & David both drove it – standard shift and all.

One time I had the car parked out in the front yard overnight only to come out the next morning and find that someone had "egged" it. Luckily I was able with some "elbow grease" to buff out the lacquer finish.

Basically, I had to be out of my mind to have ever sold this car. One major reason I sold it was that we were making a permanent move to the new home that we had built in the Florida Keys, just 21 miles back from Key West. What does that have to do with selling the TR-6? You might think that it would be the perfect car for the Keys. Nope. Only tourists rent and run around (turning beat red at week's end) in convertibles. Residents know better!

Miata

Cissie and I bought this 1997, British Racing Green, Miata on a rainy evening in Melbourne, FL, where I was conducting a workshop for Patrick Airforce Base. It came complete with "pop up" head lights. Yes, I know that the picture shows a slightly later model of the car without pop-ups.

It was really a fun car to drive, but after moving north from our home near Crystal River, Florida, we had no place to store it at Indian Lake, PA. Wish we still had it. What is nice is that many used Miatas are available – very tempting!

When I put the car up for sale, I had a young couple drive up from Washington, DC, to see it. The car was in the garage, and the young man leaned in the driver's side to examine the interior. Held in the waistband at the small of his back was a pistol! He noted that I saw the gun and announced that he worked with Homeland Security. He then produced ID to confirm his claim. He bought the car right then and there.

When we got the Miata, the joke was that if you wanted to have oil leak spots on the garage floor beneath the Miata, just like was the case with most British sports cars, you would have to physically squirt oil there using an oilier squirt can. The Japanese car engines were simply built "tighter" than their British counterparts.

The car was flawless.

Mercury Capri

This made-in-Germany Mercury Capri looked like a mini-Mustang. This picture looks a bit washed out, but it really was a deep British Racing Green in color. It had simulated leather beige bucket seats, front and back, a long hood, sunroof, and a 4-speed on the floor.

If the then new on the market Ford Mustang looked terribly sexy, then the Mercury Capri was clearly its equal. The Capri, of course, never sold as well as a Mustang, but then again, older people frequented Lincoln / Mercury dealers and may have been less receptive to a Mustang-looking sports car.

We traded our 1968 VW Bug in on it in Greensburg, PA. Prior to the official trade-in, we had been told what the official trade-in value would be. Because the car was made in Germany and had to be ordered, it was two months before it arrived. At that time the salesman said," We can't give you same trade-in now as we could have two months ago." He checked the BlueBook and the VW value had not fallen! You win some; you lose some!

We used the Capri to "haul" a 20' Ensenada sailboat.

Mercury Capri

I bought this car from a Behrend College colleague. It was built in Melbourne, Australia, where my wife, Cissie, and I visited the plant while I was at Melbourne University for a 7-month sabbatical. It was powered by a Mazda engine with a turbocharger and was the "fastest" little car I have ever driven.

I wrecked it while heading to Gannon University to teach. A car turned in front of me and I t-boned another car. Airbag went off. Everyone was "fine." Sad ending to the car, though. It was totaled!

This car was Ford's competition to the front wheel drive Mazda Capri. The Capri did not have a chance. When one thinks "sports cars" one thinks of rear wheel drive vehicles – MGs, Corvettes, Mustangs, Miatas, etc.

The "after picture!

Subaru

This was the first front wheel drive car that I had ever owned. With lots of snow in Erie, Pa, this little Subaru was up to the task – even better than our 1968 VW Bug. At the time, only three front wheel auto choices existed – Audi Fox, Oldsmobile Toronado, and Subaru. The Audi Fox was out because there was no Audi leader in Erie. The Toronado was out because it was way too big and expensive.

We purchased the car new, complete with a trailer hitch installed, for only $2,400. The car had inside (near the engine instead of out at the wheels) disk front brakes.

They say that animals know when something is missing in their diet and, hence, seek that something. I am going to assume that our hyper Irish Setter, Dublin, thought he was missing vinyl and foam rubber in his diet. While visiting my cousin Judy, we left Dublin in the Subaru with the windows partially open. When we came out after a short visit, the back seat was "missing." No, no one stole it, Dublin just destroyed it right down to the seat frame.

Apparently, this same dog had a "feather" deficiency, too, in his diet. When in grad school we lived in a 10' X 45' trailer with the living room in the front. The four couch cushions were, and I stress "were," stuffed with feathers. We came home one afternoon, opened the door, and were greeted with feathers a foot deep. To this day I do not know how so many feathers ever got stuffed in those four cushions.

Cissie and I "camped" in this car while traveling in Canada. The man at the campground asked, "Where are you planning to sleep?" "Right here in the back," we said. Cissie and I were a bit more limbered then!

On one trip to Niagara Falls we pulled off the side of the road above the falls, more than 100' above the river. There was a three-foot high stone wall separating the parking area from the over-looking cliff. In order to let Dublin stretch his legs, we opened the Subaru's hatch and out he bounded right up on the top of that stone wall and off it to the cliff area beyond.

All we could think of was what are we going to tell Bob's mother about her beloved "grand-dog" leaping to his death. What we didn't know was that on other side of that stone wall, out of sight from either us or Dublin, was a fifteen-foot area next to the cliff. Dublin, of course, had no way of knowing this when he made is almost fateful leap.

The car rusted like crazy! The story going around was that the Japanese had taken all the steel that we had dropped on them in WWII and used it to build their cars. Still, it was a fun car to drive.

Subaru

Two door coupe where our two kids, when it rained, would argue about who would sit where in the backseat. Dad (me) would be standing there, holding open the door, getting drenched. This was our first and last two-door family car! A rule was formed – David sits behind Dad. Rebecca sits behind Mom. Problem solved.

Keeping with Subaru tradition at that time, the fenders literally rusted off. Subaru actually sent us two new ones. Lots of trips to University Park for Senate meetings!

This car served me well on many, many trips from Erie, PA, to State College, PA (Penn State University), and back as I was taking courses towards my Superintendent's Letter of Eligibility.

The Subaru's front wheel drive came in real useful for the snowy trips.

The picture below was taken on the wharf at the foot of State Street in Erie, PA. Presque Isle is seen across the bay.

Subaru 4WD

This was my First 4WD (4-wheel drive) vehicle. I could not believe how well this little car could negotiate the snow in Erie, PA. You simply pulled up a lever to engage the 4WD and drove on – no matter the weather. This car would go anywhere in the snow. Again, keeping up the tradition of the previous Subarus, it was prone to rust – mostly to the frame rather than to body panels. Despite this, we loved the car. Son, David, had a bit of a "bang" backing it into the garage.

Subaru Forrester

Not a lot to say about this car. I bought it in 2012 in Johnstown, PA, but was not satisfied with the seat covers. They always seem "wrinkled." I know, this sounds like a "Micky Mouse" sort of complaint, but the poor seat quality stood out to me each time I got in the car.

While vacationing in St. Augustine, FL, we traded it on a 2012, CR-V with all the bells and whistles. Got a very good trade-in.

Saturn

It was one of the first Saturn cars in Erie, PA. I had to buy it in Buffalo because there was no Erie dealer. A dealer was promised, but one never appeared.

It was an inexpensive, standard shift, "plastic" (no rust) car. Amazingly, it came standard with 4-wheel disk brakes.

Later, kids drove it, and then Becky took it to medical school. Son, David, "blew out" two tires and damaged two wheels while accidently hopping an unseen curb. Cissie and I returned home from a trip only to see the car up on blocks in our driveway with a note from #1 son explaining the situation. He took care of it all.

Saturn ION

We bought this very inexpensive car in Gainesville, Florida. It had every bell & whistle that Saturn offered, including leather. The problem was that the front seats were terrible – very, very uncomfortable. It is too bad that Saturn ignored this crucial area of comfort, one of the first features any owner / driver would notice.

I returned the car to the dealer within a month (under 1000 miles) and got back *all* my money (including my GM points). This is when Saturn had its "return it within a month" program if you were not satisfied. Note, Saturn is now out of business. I hope that we were not partially responsible for its demise.

Toyota Corolla

A *Plain Jane* car but comfortable, roomy and dependable. It had great gas mileage for my many trips back and forth from Crystal River to Gainesville (UF) where I taught as an Adjunct Professor at the University of Florida's graduate school. It had lots of room inside, including the backseat, and loads of space in the trunk.

Seriously, if you look up "dull" in the dictionary it probably says, "see Corolla." But there is no doubt that Toyota has got it right with Corolla because they keep on churning them out.

Cissie and I saw it being traded in at a local Toyota dealer. Immediately bought it. Toyota just keeps making these cars, and I hope they never stop.

Toyota Prius

A big THANKS to Toyota for taking the risk to bring out the Prius. If they had not taken the chance, where would we be today with hybrid, and later, total electric cars? Our Prius was one of the very first ones sold.

The Prius changed driving as we know it. By careful driving, we could get just over 60 mpg. Not bad! Comfortable & stylish car. Might look like a compact car but was classified as a mid-size vehicle.

American car makers at the time shied away from the challenge of hybrids. But, as you may recall, General Motors actually beat the Prius to the punch. GM brought out their two passengers, 1996, EV1 and leased them to customers, including to several famous movie stars.

But, because GM was making much more money selling large Hummers, they decided to cancel *ALL* EV1 leases – even for those who wanted to buy their leased car outright. GM scooped up all the EV1s, sometimes in the dead of night, and disposed of them. For your viewing pleasure (or displeasure) see the video titled, *Who Killed the Electric Car?*

Scion xB

My 2003 Scion xB was simply the ***most fun*** to drive car I have ever owned – including my various sports cars! Let me say this again. The Scion xB was simply the ***most fun*** to drive car I have ever owned. It was like driving a go-kart!

It was boxy, by design, had five doors, easy to get in and out of, had a minimalist yet functional dashboard, seated 4 or 5 adults comfortably, had power everything, and came equipped with either a 5-speed or automatic transmission.

I almost flew out to the west coast to buy one because, initially, they were only available there. Instead, we waited until they were available on the east coast. Very, very roomy, great gas mileage, and still a "head turner." I may get another one!

Unfortunately, Scion decided to come out with a second generation xB which was bigger, heavier, and had a larger engine, all of which translated into relatively poor gas mileage and less of the "go kart" fun driving experience.

Now, as of 2015, the car is gone, and it seems as if Toyota has simply turned that market over to the popular Kia Soul. A very big mistake on their part.

Toyota Sienna

What can I say? One of the best car decisions Cissie and I ever made – followed only by our 2nd Sienna. Roomy, dependable, a joy to drive. Long distance travel miles just melted away.

When we traded this 1998 van in 2005, it still ran and felt like a new car.

Toyota Sienna

Everything about our 1998 Sienna applies here, too. Best all-around vehicle we have ever owned. Over 15 years old, with just shy of 180,000 miles, our 2005 is still going strong. At some point we may buy a newer one (not "new"- too much money). Any leads on a newer one?

Cissie and I could literally drive for 700 miles or more, all the time listening to books-on-CD and arrive refreshed.

Note, this car has an AM & FM radio, a cassette player, *AND* a CD player. Try finding that combination on today's vehicles! Even our neighbor's brand-new Cadillac does not have these audio conveniences.

I transported most of the materials we used to remodel our Indian Lake, PA, house in, or on top of, this van. If I told you all the things that we carried or pulled with the van you would probably call 911 and report me for van abuse. I would have to plead "guilty as charged." We also used it to haul our pontoon boat and trailer, and our cargo trailer. It never "complained."

The van was a trooper when we needed it and a bit of luxury when we wanted that. Still, today, those riding in the Sienna repeatedly think that it is "new" and not 15 years old.

Honda CR-V

We have always been a Toyota family, but when my sister-in-law, Patty, was ready to sell her 2000 CR-V 4WD, we couldn't pass it up. She kept it garaged and in good shape having completed all the dealer recommended service over the years.

This car would go anywhere in snow & was so very comfortable. We had a second set of rims/snow tires for it – making easy winter/spring and fall/winter changes possible. The car even had a small "removable "picnic" table in the spare tire area.

Honda CR-V

Honda has a winner in its CR-Vs – any year. Our 2012 is the top of the line and looks as good, today, as when it left the showroom.

As I look in our neighborhood, it seems as if Honda must be giving these cars away for free. Everyone is buying one! But here is a problem alert! Our neighbor across the street bought a 2018, and, while preparing for a trip where he planned to make use of books-on-CD from the library, found out that his car had no CD player!

This is shortsighted in that young, hip to all kinds of electronic devices, do not buy CRVs. Middle age (and older) people buy them, and the last thing they want to do is to sign-out CDs from the library, take them home, "burn" them onto a thumb drive and then, finally, be ready to travel.

Honda Element

    I had always wanted a Honda Element, so I bought a used one in Florida. Simply amazing the amount of room, especially headroom. Ended up selling it within a year because I had no place to store it inside once we relocated to our home at Indian Lake, PA.

    The rear doors were a pain because, to open them, you first had to open one of the front doors. I had planned to do a bit of conversion to the car and make it a camper for periodic trips. But how do you open the back-side suicide doors when sleeping in the back if the front doors must be opened first?

Acura TSX

I "thought" my driving van days were over, so I bought a 4-dr Acura TSX. I was wrong. Within a month I had traded it for our 2005 Sienna – and have never been happier. To Acura's credit, I received a trade-in equal to *exactly* what I had paid for it despite Ed, Cissie's father, grazing the rear bumper with his van just before the official trade-in! Surprise, surprise.

Lincoln Continental

Tom and Peggy bought a new Volvo S60 and traded in their Continental with not all that high mileage. We bought it right away from the Volvo dealer. Decided, once again, that I am not a four-door sedan guy! Not long after, we sold the car.

I was able to sell the Lincoln for more money than its cost from the dealer. We used the extra money to screen in our front porch in Beverly Hills, FL.

Ford Pickup
(with snowplow)

I bought a used Ford pickup, added a used snowplow, and was ready for the snow that covered our very long and wind-swept driveway in North East, PA. The pickup, with the snow blade lowered, would "just" fit in our garage with the garage door barely clearing – all ready to blast away the snow.

Although I had a dependable 12hp Sears tractor (not just lawn mower) with a snow blade,

without the power of the pickup to move the snow,
I would have been lost.

Ford Van

I bought this used, 1976, 6-cylinder, standard shift, Ford van. It was several years old at the time. I took it to Ohio where they cut out a large portion of the roof and installed a "pop up" roof with 6' 2" headroom. This allowed me to store the van inside my garage, easily clearing the garage door opening.

I then converted the inside of the van into a camper with sleeping areas for the family. Sleeping spaces were altered as time went by in order to accommodate our two kids' growth. This was the vehicle that got me "hooked" on vans.

When Becky was very young, she slept in an area just below the pop-up roof. Once, when checking on her at our camp site, I opened the van door and found her asleep on the floor! I suppose she tumbled there.

Later I built two areas for sleeping that looked like a dresser drawer with the drawers removed. In David's case, as he grew taller and taller (i.e., longer and longer) I had to cut out the end "wall" for his feet to protrude through.

I arm-wrestled the car salesman for the antenna for the van. Yep – I won. At least that is how I remember it!

I used the van to haul, launch and retrieve my 20' Ensenada sailboat. Because, at first, there were only the two front seats, this made retrieving the boat rather easy – or so I thought. One day, after sailing until late afternoon, I hopped off at the dock and went to get the van and trailer. My brother stayed on the boat and, after my opening the back doors and backing the trailer down the boat ramp, he guided the boat onto the trailer. I set the van's emergency brake, swiveled around, and "walked" back through the empty van to hook the boat to the trailer. Uh Oh!

As I "walked" back, I noticed that there was water inching its way forward onto the floor of the van. Apparently the van and trailer (with the boat) were sliding down the slippery ramp into the lake. Almost too late I realized that the emergency brake only works on the rear wheels, the wheels on the slippery boat ramp. I "ran" forward and slammed my foot on the van's brake (which worked on all 4 wheels) and stopped it sliding further. Luckily, the son of the man who managed the park came along with his 4-wheel drive truck and was able to pull the van, the trailer and the boat out of the water!

One summer we traveled to West Palm Beach to visit Cissie's dad. To save money, we stayed in campgrounds. One night, in Georgia, it was so hot that Cissie got so many insect bites that the next day we went to Sears and bought a 5000 btu air conditioner. That night, with the air conditioner "installed" in the Ford's passenger door window, we all slept well.

The very next day we made it back to Erie and to make use of the air conditioner, installed it in our bedroom window. But, we had no real need for it. So, basically two months after buying the air conditioner in Georgia, we returned it, no questions asked, to Sears.

Normally I did most of the driving, but occassionally Cissie would take over on stretches of road such as a Turnpike. I vividly recall Cissie driving, while dad (me) and our two young children, David and Rebecca, sacked out on the rear full sized "bed" as the air rushed by (from the front windows through the van and out the rear windows) and the van gently swayed from side to side. Wow!

The picture below shows us all set for camping with a storage box hanging off the rear door and two bicycles (out of sight) that hung off the front bumper.

Ford E-150 Van

We continued our love of vans by purchasing this 1986 Ford. It, believe it or not, was 4-on-the-floor stick shift and had two, yes two, gas tanks. Being only 6 cylinders, it really had the range. Ours was gray, not red.

Our actual van has large windows on both sides to which we added shades for privacy when needed. I had these windows installed. By removing the rear bench seat, still leaving seating for four, we could carry all our necessary travel and camping gear.

I really liked the car except for one situation. I had been driving standard shift vehicles all my life and, thus, had no difficulty with the 4-on-the-floor stick shift of this van. But, at about 60,000 miles, the clutch started to shimmy, slip, and shake.

I contacted Ford and they said that I was somehow at fault. Note, I had long since left behind my teenage driving habits where no doubt I had "mistreated" a car here or there. It just seemed odd that a supposedly rugged E-150 van, often a vehicle that would have been purchased and used (perhaps abused) by construction workers, would have clutch trouble at only 60,000 miles.

This situation pushed me away from Ford and over to Toyota vans.

Dodge Roadtrek 190

Purchased from Ferd, our St. Augustine condo landlord. I altered the insides to, among other things, enable sleeping front to back rather than sideways.

Believe it or not, the 19' Roadtrek had 6' 2" headroom, a full kitchen, toilet with shower, and lots more. It drove like a dream. Cissie always took a stand-up shower while I normally trotted to the campground shower and toilet.

Traveling in the RV saved us a lot of hotel or motel costs and insured that we were sleeping each night in our own clean bed. State parks were our favorites.

This van had 160,000 miles on it when I bought it, but it drove just fine. Over the time that I had the RV the only problem was a water pump leak that necessitated installing an inexpensive rebuilt pump.

I did significant work on the inside of the RV, in effect, changing it from a Roadtrek Versitile version to a Roadtrek Popular version. The change consisted of changing the sleeping arrangements from one bed across the back to two beds, one along each side of the rear of the van.

This accomplished two things. One, it allowed my wife and I to have our own bed separated by a middle of the aisle walkway – great for having to get up to go potty at night. Two, it allowed my bed to accommodate my 6'2" height (length). Many other features, too, were changed.

The Dodge 318 motor is a trooper and can, if needed, be easily repaired by most any mechanic. We simply loved the RV. Although we sold it when moving to The Villages, FL, (storage problem), we are looking for another one! Wish us luck.

1997 Roadtrek Versatile

Volkswagen
Westfalia

Saw it while riding my motorcycle. Gave the owner $10 to "hold" it. It had had virtually no use at all. The owner had three cars and only a two-car garage where the VW took up one of the spaces. This VW, even then, stickered for just over $25,000! I bought it for about half that amount.

I drove it to the Florida Keys with brother Randy, one time, and with a teaching colleague, another time. A very "cool" car that is worth its weight in gold, now!

Twice, the Westphalia would not start, and I had no idea why. It seemed like the battery was weak. When it happened in Florida, I took it into Sears for a checkup. When the mechanic checked the battery area (a box behind the passenger seat), he found that the battery had "leaked" acid. Actually it had not "leaked." I had accidently used too long of screws when attaching something to the front side of the battery box. The screws poked a hole in the side of the battery. My bad!

As nice as the camper was, especially that it had air conditioning, the problem was that the air conditioner was clear in the back and my wife and I were clear in the front! Further, you would not want to have a front-end accident because there was literally nothing between you and whatever you might hit – the engine, of course, was in the rear.

Do not be scared by the two mountain-looking men in the picture. They are my brother, Randy, and my nephew, Tim, enjoying camping in the great outdoors, at Cooks Forest, PA. It looks as if we brought with us more than Lewis and Clark did for their expedition!

PASSAGE

We bought this 26' RV from a FL State Policeman who lived in Jacksonville. Basically, it had never been used except for sleeping. Spotlessly clean.

We drove it to the KEYS and the very next week the price of gasoline *Skyrocketed* to $1.60 a gallon. Compounding matters was the fact that RVs were not permitted to be stored on our lot. Put an ad at ACE Hardware and sold it within a week!

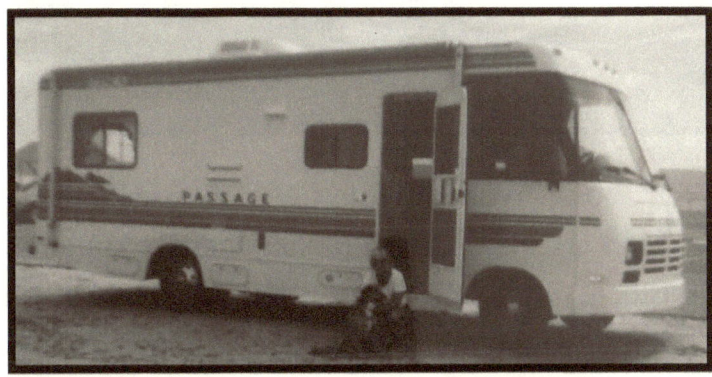

VW Vista

Wow! What a find! Saw it at a dealer along the road in FL. Stopped, negotiated, bought it right then and there. Sadly, I left our friends Tom & Peggy waiting at restaurant. They were not at all happy! It was the perfect RV.

It had a VW front end and a Winnebago rear. Thus, it got terrific gas mileage and, yet, had full headroom, a full kitchen, toilet, shower, generator, etc. Ginger, our dog, loved traveling in it.

It was the perfect size for the three (i.e., Ginger) of us. I could easily fit into most parking spots and, with a little help from Cissie, back into many parallel parking spots. With just two axles, turnpike fees were kept to a minimum.

The Vista had a fold-out couch that made a fair size bed, while still permitting one to pass by for those to the potty nighttime trips. It also had a queen size bed over the top of the cab.

Add Cissie making coffee and toast in the morning in the Vista, and me cooking bacon and eggs on the picnic table, and it does not get much better than that.

On more than one occasion we would drive to a beach with an ocean view, orient our "picture window" on the passenger side of the RV, make a few drinks and just enjoy the sunset. Once, while in upper Canada, we parked just on the edge of a cliff looking out over the Atlantic. With a campfire blazing, Ginger by our side, it was the definition of "relaxing."

Not to be indelicate, but when stuck in traffic, it was comforting to know that the potty was right there with us, and the fridge with cold soft drinks and lunch meat was even closer.

We want the Vista back!

VW Bug

Yes, that is our Irish Setter, Sheridan's Dublin Malone (Dubby), sticking his head out through the sunroof. He was a bit hyper!

Bought the VW Bug in 1968. It had a sunroof. It was stick shift and was lots of fun to drive. We took it to grad school at Penn State.

Interestingly, I traded my 1965 MGB on the VW Bug when I got married. My friend, Steve Tomaino, traded his MGB on a VW Bug when he got married. My other buddy, Fuzzy Knight, traded his MGB in on – no, not a VW Bug - but instead a flashy Fiat 124 Spider convertible. Fuzzy did not get married – at least not just then.

My VW Bug had a "gas" heater positioned under the front hood taking up about 1/3 of that area that normally would be used as a "trunk." The heater was so efficient that, literally, once turned on, by the time you backed to the end of the driveway you had to turn it down. Normally lots of heat was not something associated with an air-cooled VW Bug.

Several times when I would pull into a gas station to fill up, I would turn off the car and the gas heater would backfire. It was so loud at times that those around the car would "hit the deck."

I used to use a joke in class when I taught a section on statistics. I would tell the students that my VW Bug was extremely reliable – especially on cold winter mornings. The class thought I meant that it would *always* start, but what I meant was that it would *never* start – hence it was reliable. I could always count on it. I always received a groan.

Suzuki Samurai

Purchased this car from my brother, Randy's, neighbor. In great condition with 3 canvas top versions. Ginger, our dog, and I traveled from Erie to the Keys with the car fully loaded – and I mean fully loaded.

It had a chrome push bar in the front that I added. It added a "hairy" look if that is possible with a Suzuki.

It was a perfect "Florida Keys" car. You felt like a "local" while driving it, although it was a bit of a bumpy ride for Ed, Cissie's dad, when driving back and forth from Cudjoe Key to Key West.

In October, Key West celebrates *Fantasy Fest,* a celebration not unlike Mardi Gras in New Orleans. It definitely is NOT for children. Many slightly inebriated fun goers get their bodies 'air brushed' and move about, topless – or less!

How does this relate to the Suzuki? Well, a highlight of the celebration is a parade down Duval Street whereby we decorated the Suzuki and found our place in line immediately behind a panel truck that had very large screens attached to the rear and to both sides. On the roof of the van stood someone with a camera on a tripod taking *very* up close pictures of the revelers, especially the semi-nude ones, lining the street. Those life-size pictures were displayed for me in living color just three feet from my front bumper. It is a wonder that I could keep my eyes on the road!

Opel Manta

Bought car from a colleague who kept it in England for his repeated trips there. He bought it back from me at the end of my 1984/85 sabbatical at Durham University. Although not considered a lot of miles, today, the car had 80,000 miles on it.

During one of our children's school holidays, we drove it to the continent and on to Berlin where the "wall" was still up. Very scary. At the time one had to drive through East Germany in order to reach West Berlin and then repeat the return trip when leaving Berlin. It was a very sobering portion of the trip.

On the return home, the engine overheated at the Arc de Triomphe, Paris. Here we were at the base of the Arc with our hood up, steam coming out of the radiator, and 12 lanes of traffic streaming into the roundabout.

Awhile later, I had just returned from Paris with a group of Durham University faculty and students and phoned Cissie to come and pick me up at the University. She announced, "I have good news and I have bad news. The good news is that we have a new car. The bad news was that the suspension on the Opel had snapped off." The scary part was that this could have happened a month earlier when we were driving through East Germany on our way into and out of West Berlin. All got fixed!

Used the Opel to visit lots of B&Bs, youth hostels, and castles – and still more castles! The kids seemed to have many school holidays, and we took advantage of them all to travel.

Ford Cortina

I bought this standard shift car while on sabbatical in Melbourne, Australia in 1992. It was "orange" in color. Great car. Wish I could have brought it back to the USA. Sold it to a neighbor.

The car salesman took me up to the AA (their version of our AAA) where I was able to purchase seven months of car insurance for just $75.00.

Although this car did not come to the States, it was very popular in England and Australia, especially in road racing.

Cadillac Sedan DeVille

Margaret, Cissie's mom, willed this car to me. It was a joy to drive. Sold it when Cissie and I relocated to the Keys.

I used to get some "ribbing" from my colleagues regarding my driving such a large, gas guzzling, car. But the fact is, I lived just 1 mile from campus and, thus, used far less gas than those driving smaller cars who had to drive across (and back home) Erie to reach campus.

It was so big, yet so easy to drive. I loved it.

Jaguar XKE

Bob's *Dream* Car. When anyone ever says, "I want such and such………" I respond by saying, "I want a yellow Jaguar XKE, too, but you don't see one parked in my driveway!" By the way, I would be just as happy with a red JAG, too.

Thanks for joining me on my ride down memory lane!

Have fun! Have more fun!

Remember, "Fun is nature's reward for learning!"

Books by Dr. Robert T. Tauber, PhD

1. *Projecting Enthusiasm: The Key to Dynamic Presentations for Professionals!*
2. *Delivering Empathy: Fundamental to Successful Leadership!*
3. *Praise Less, Encourage More: Judge, Evaluate and Manipulate Less; Fortify, Galvanize, Embolden and Influence More!*
4. *Inheritance? What Inheritance? We spent it on travel, food, and drink!*
5. *Oral Communication Skills for the Vocational & Technology Workforce: Walk the Walk and Especially Talk the Talk!*
6. *Yorkshire Pudding, Castles, B&Bs and Pubs: An American Family's 1984-85 Sabbatical in England!*
7. *Using Empathy as Physicians: The What, Why, and How!*
8. *From Whence We Came: The Tauber Family History in Photos.*
9. *Giving Children the "Expectations Advantage": Make the Power of Expectations Work for You!*
10. *Classroom Management: "A" to "Z" Discipline Strategies: Simple Strategies that WILL Improve Classroom Discipline!*
11. *Negative Reinforcement & Time-Out: Two POSITIVE Classroom Management Strategies.*

12. *Classroom Management: Sound Theory and Effective Practice* (4th ed).

13. *Acting Lessons for Teachers: Using Performance Skills in the Classroom.*

14. *Self-Fulfilling Prophecy: A Practical Guide to Its Use in Education.*

15. *Bob's "AUTO" Biography: Are Cars a Reflection of One's Personality?*

The majority of these books are low cost, easily read and a bit fun to read, informative, and immediately useful. They are available by going to Amazon.com, selecting "books," and then typing in "Robert T. Tauber." Also available as ebooks.

rtt1453@comcast.net

www.ingramcontent.com/pod-product-compliance
Lightning Source LLC
Chambersburg PA
CBHW030727180526

45157CB00008BA/3080